SCIENCE FILES

ROCKS AND MINERALS

SCIENCE FILES – ROCKS AND MINERALS
was produced by

David West 🧍🧍 **Children's Books**

7 Princeton Court
55 Felsham Road
London SW15 1AZ

Designers: Rob Shone, Fiona Thorne, David West
Editor: James Pickering
Picture Research: Carrie Haines

First published in Great Britain in 2001 by
Heinemann Library, Halley Court, Jordan Hill,
Oxford OX2 8EJ, a division of Reed Educational and
Professional Publishing Limited.

OXFORD MELBOURNE AUCKLAND
JOHANNESBURG BLANTYRE GABORONE
IBADAN PORTSMOUTH (NH) USA CHICAGO

Copyright © 2001 David West Children's Books

05 04 03 02 01
10 9 8 7 6 5 4 3 2 1

ISBN 0 431 14312 9 (HB)
ISBN 0 431 14313 7 (PB)

British Library Cataloguing in Publication Data

Parker, Steve, 1952 -
Rocks & minerals. - (Science files)
1. Rocks 2. Minerals
I. Title
553

Printed and bound in Spain by Bookprint, S.L., Barcelona

PHOTO CREDITS :
Abbreviations: t-top, m-middle, b-bottom, r-right,
l-left.

Front cover - bl - Vaughan Fleming, Science Photo
Library, m - Mary Evans Picture Library, br (@ 98
Lester) - The Stock Market. 4b (Krafft), 5bl, 24bl,
25mr & br (Vaughan Fleming), 6tl (John Mead), 6
(Jerry Schod), 7br (George Roos/Peter Arnold Inc),
(Nancy Sefton), 8t (E.R. Degginger), 9bl (G.
Bradlewis), 9tr 17tl (Alex Bartel), 10m (David
Hardy), 11tl (ONES, 1986 Distribution SPOT Imag
11mr (David Parker), 12b (Tony Craddock), 12/13
(Martin Bond), 14tr (Colin Cuthbert), 16ml & 26/2
(David Nanuk), 20bl (Chris Knapton), 20/21t (Eye
Science), 21m (Rosenfeld Images Ltd), 22tr (Franço
Sauze), 22mr (Klaus Guldgrandsen), 23br (James
King-Holmes), 28bl (Simon Fraser) - Science Photo
Library. 14bl (Upperhall Ltd), 15tr (J.J. Travel &
Photography), 24tr (Tony Whitham), 29tl - Robert
Harding Picture Library. 10bl, 19mr (British
Museum), 27bl - Ann Ronan Picture Library. 6/7b,
15br, 22bl - Mary Evans Picture Library. 5br (@ 98
Lester), 12m (@ 98 Georgina Bowater) - The Stock
Market. 16tr - Scancem. 18/19t - Villeroy & Boch.
19bl Waterford Wedgwood.

Every effort has been made to trace the copyright
holders and we apologise in advance for any
unintentional omissions. We would be pleased to
insert the appropriate acknowledgement in any
subsequent edition of this publication.

*An explanation of difficult words can be
found in the glossary on page 30.*

SCIENCE FILES

ROCKS AND MINERALS

Steve Parker

Heinemann
LIBRARY

CONTENTS

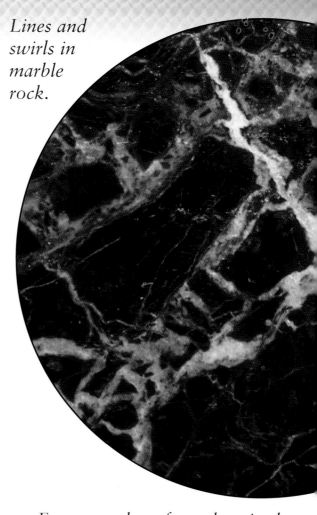

Lines and swirls in marble rock.

Enormous heat from deep in the Earth makes rocks melt and flow li syrup, as lava from volcanoes.

INTRODUCTION

More than one million years ago, early people chipped rocks to make simple tools such as stone axes and scrapers. More than 20,000 years ago, people ground up minerals from rocks, and mixed them with plant and animal juices, to make coloured paints for beautiful pictures on cave walls. Today, hundreds of kinds of rocks, and thousands of types of minerals, are used in countless ways, for objects and items that vary from a building brick to a diamond ring.

We dig up vast amounts of rocks and minerals every year. But the Earth's supplies are not endless. Such raw materials must be used with care and recycled wherever possible.

...ne of the world's most precious items is ...glistening, sparkling diamond. Yet this is ...simple mineral made by natural ...ocesses in the Earth's rocks.

From ancient times, people shaped or carved rocks to make statues. These giant heads on Easter Island, in the Pacific, each weigh more than a juggernaut truck.

Beneath our feet, the outer layer of the Earth is made of naturally hard, tough substances called rocks.

TYPES OF ROCKS

There are many kinds of rocks, such as flint, sandstone, limestone, marble, slate, granite and basalt. Each has its own colour, hardness, heaviness and texture.

Amethyst

Chalcedony

Some caves contain pointe icicle-like shapes made fro minerals, left as water drip from the roof or on to the floor. Stalagmites rise up (here), stalactites hang dow

Most minerals form shapes known as crystals, with flat sides and angled edges. The minerals below are prized for their colours and patterns. When they are smoothed and polished, they shine and sparkle.

Agate

Lapis lazuli

Turquoise

Amber

Opal

WHAT ARE MINERALS?

Each mineral contains a combination of the simplest natural substances of all. These substances are called chemical elements. For example, the mineral calcite, or calcium carbonate, is made up of one part of the chemical element calcium (Ca), one part carbon (C), and three parts oxygen (O). So the symbol for the mineral calcite is $CaCO_3$.

Facts from the **PAST**

Each type of rock or stone has certain features that make it useful in some way. A lump or nodule of flint cracks or splits when hit, into thin, sharp-edged pieces. Flint was one of the first rocks to be shaped by careful hammering like this, into tools such as scrapers and cutters, and weapons like spear heads and daggers.

Flint arrow heads 4,000 years old.

WHAT ARE ROCKS MADE OF?

ocks are made of basic natural ubstances called minerals. Each rock as its own mixture or combination f minerals. Limestone, the rock hich forms white cliffs, contains ainly one mineral, known as calcite.

THE ROCK CYCLE

Earth's rocks may seem strong enough to last for ever. But they do not. Very slowly, they change. They are worn away by the weather, and they are squashed and melted by huge forces deep within the Earth. Gradually old rocks are destroyed and new ones form. This is called the rock cycle.

Lava from a volcano may take years to go cool and hard.

Lava (molten rock on the surface) cools and goes solid, forming igneous rock

Great heat near magma changes original rock into new metamorphic rock

Magma (molten rock underground)

In warm shallow seas, small, soft coral creatures make hard mineral cups around themselves. These build into coral reef rocks.

BREAKING DOWN

Even the hardest rocks are worn down over thousands of years, by the forces of nature. These include the hot sun, freezing ice, rain, snow, glaciers, waves, and winds carrying sand and dust. This wearing down is known as erosion.

Ideas for the FUTURE

When rock becomes very hot (usually 1,000°C or more), it melts and goes runn This is why lava oozes or spurts from a volcano. If the flowing lava could be led into box-like shapes or moulds, it would cool and go solid in the shape of the mould. When the block shapes of rock a tipped out – instant building bricks!

The three main kinds of rocks are made in different ways. Igneous rocks form when molten (melted) rock cools and hardens. Metamorphic rocks form as great heat and pressure change, or metamorphose, one type of rock into another, without melting. Sedimentary rocks form as pieces or particles of rocks settle in layers, known as sediments, then become squeezed and naturally glued together.

ocks are eroded (worn own) into small particles by nd, rain, waves, ice and sun

Particles of rock are blown by the wind, and carried by rivers into the sea

Rock particles sink, press together and form layers of sedimentary rock

Great pressure far underground changes original rock into new metamorphic rock

On the coast, waves crash against the rocks and erode shapes such as arches.

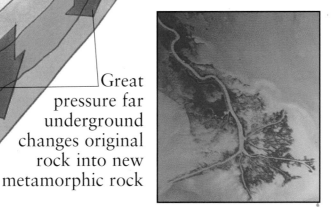

Mud and other particles settle at river mouths, like the Mississippi.

BUILDING UP

The forces of nature destroy old rocks. But the mineral particles are not lost. Huge amounts of heat and pressure squash or even melt these tiny pieces. Other minerals work like natural glue to stick them together. The results are huge, hard lumps of new rock – and so the cycle goes on.

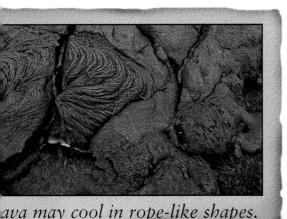

ava may cool in rope-like shapes.

Rocks are everywhere – bare and exposed on the ground, or under soil and plants. But not all rocks are rich in minerals, or suitable for uses such as building. Scientists known as geologists must search for the useful rocks.

EYES IN THE SKIES

Geologists start to find suitable rocks by studying photographs taken by satellites or high-flying planes. Different types of rocks can be recognized from their colour and surface appearance.

Survey satellites such as SPOT circle Earth and take pictures of the ground and rock

Facts from the **PAST**

Many times over the years, people have quickly gathered at a certain place, when precious minerals are found there – especially gems like diamond. These 'jewel rushes' cause buildings and whole towns to spring up in remote places like deserts, mountains, swamps and forests.

Diamond rush in South Africa, 1895.

ROCK SHOCK

When a train or truck passes close by, you m feel the ground shake. The movements or vibrations from the train or truck travel through the rocks in tl ground. Stronger shoc or seismic waves do th same. Their speed, and the way they fade in strength or deflect (change direction), sho the types and layers of rocks under the surfac

TESTS AT THE SITE

When photographs reveal suitable rocks, geologists travel to the area for on-site studies. They use mini-explosions or 'thumper' machines to see how shock waves travel through the ground (see below). They also drill into the rocks and remove small pieces, or samples, to take back to the laboratory for further tests.

Satellite pictures of the Lout Desert, Iran (above) and the mountains of the Himalayas (left) show patterns and colours. These indicate rocks rich in certain minerals.

The vibro-truck has a large plate between the wheels, which sends shock waves through the ground to find rocks.

e seismic waves are made explosives or vibrating achines. Rows of delicate nsors detect them, and a mputer shows the results.

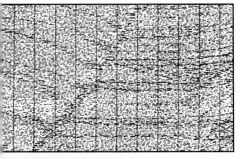

int-out of a seismic survey.

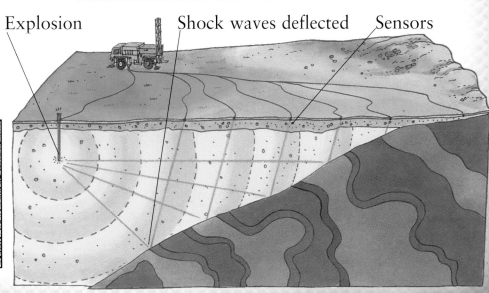

Explosion   Shock waves deflected   Sensors

Mines are places where minerals, or rocks rich in them, are dug out of the ground. Blocks of stone, for uses such as building, come from quarries.

MINES AT THE SURFACE

Where soft, mineral-rich rocks are at or near the Earth's surface, they are scraped up by massive excavators. Harder rocks are loosened by blasting with explosives. This is known as open-cast or open-pit mining. The rocks are usually taken away in huge trucks for the next stage, which is extracting the minerals.

Open-cast mines destroy the landscape. In many places today, they must be covered by soil and planted with trees.

Some deep min are big enough for railways an trucks. Digging continues until the mine is 'worked out' – is no longer worth digging up the rocks.

RHEINBRAUN 288

KRUPP SIEMENS

MINES BELOW GROUND

If the mineral-rich rocks are deep underground, a vertical elevator (lift) shaft is drilled or blasted downwards. Then galleries are tunnelled sideways into the rock, which is broken up and taken away. As the gallery lengthens, it may change direction, to stay in the mineral-rich band or seam of rock.

'Dimension' stone from quarry is blocks for buildings, paving slabs, statues and similar uses. 'Aggregate' stone is smaller pieces such as shingle and sand.

Ideas for the FUTURE

Here and there on the sea bed, Earth's natural processes have produced nodules – rocky lumps containing large amounts of pure minerals. Deep-sea submersible craft could gather these. It would save mining huge amounts of rocks on land, which contain much less mineral.

Gathering minerals in the deep sea.

HOLES, TUNNELS AND DREDGERS

An open-cast pit is a giant hole at the surface where mineral-rich rocks are removed. To go deeper, a vertical lift shaft leads down to galleries tunnelled into the rocks.

Some sediments (layers of small particles such as sand or mud) contain plentiful minerals. They are gathered by dredger ships or shore-based excavators.

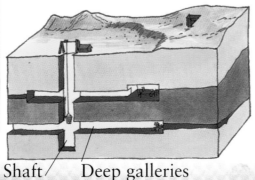
Open-cast pit

Underground mine   Shaft   Deep galleries

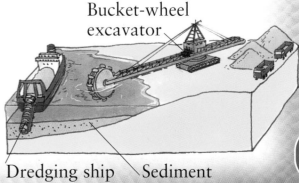
Bucket-wheel excavator

Dredging ship   Sediment

Rough, grey building bricks make walls that will not be seen. They are faced (covered) with smart red bricks

You could simply pile up lumps of rock to make walls for a house. But it would be safer to shape them into box-like blocks, for a stronger, more stable wall, or mix up clay-rich minerals, form them into box shapes, and bake them hard, to make bricks.

Coloured bricks and tiles can make decorati patterns and designs, as on the Summer Pala in Khosa, Uzbekistan, Central Asia.

THE BRICKWORKS

Special clays or shales are crushed into piece These pass through net-like screens which catch the larger lumps and send them back t the crusher. The resulting fine clay powder is mixed with additive and colouring chemicals

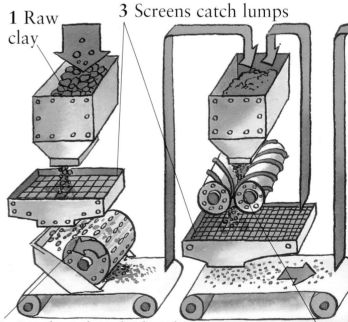

1 Raw clay

3 Screens catch lumps

2 Crushers break the clay into tiny pieces

O CRACKS OR GAPS

atural rock can be shaped or carved
 saws, chisels and other tools, into
ocks, round-edged cobbles, and
inner slabs and tiles. But the rock
ust not contain any tiny cracks, or it
uld shatter under the weight of more
ocks above. Bricks can be mass
oduced to the same quality, without
acks, and the same size, so
ey fit closely, without gaps.
ey are joined using
 other mineral product,
ment (see next page).

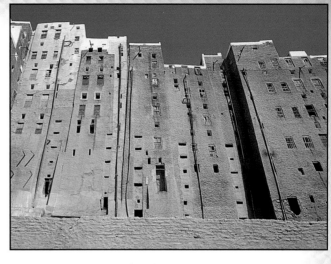

Adobe bricks are made from natural mud minerals, simply mixed and baked in the sun. These multi-storey houses in South Yemen are the world's tallest mud-brick structures.

e clay mixes with water into a
 paste, and any air bubbles are
noved. The paste is pressed into
ck-shaped moulds and the bricks
 tipped out and baked hard.

Stone street cobbles.

Facts from the PAST

Some of the world's oldest and greatest structures, the Pyramids of Ancient Egypt, were made from natural stone. There were no power saws, trucks or cranes. Gangs of people cut, shaped, dragged and lifted the blocks, each weighing many tonnes, all by hand.

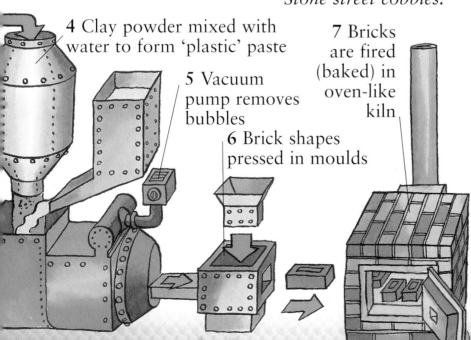

4 Clay powder mixed with water to form 'plastic' paste

5 Vacuum pump removes bubbles

6 Brick shapes pressed in moulds

7 Bricks are fired (baked) in oven-like kiln

Pyramid under construction.

One of the most important building materials in the world is cement. It is a very fine, greyish powder made from various rocks and minerals. Cement mixed with sand and water forms a paste, called mortar, which is used to stick bricks together.

Mortar or concrete can be delivered by truck, ready-mixed. But once water is added, setting begins and cannot be stopped. The truck's large rotating drum keeps the cement moving, to prevent it setting.

Making cement uses up huge amounts of raw materials and energy. More than 1,000 million tonnes are made every year.

THE CEMENT WORKS

Raw materials for cement vary, depending on the type required. It may need to be very fast-setting, or withstand chemicals such as acids, or cope with great heat.

The raw materials from hoppers are dried, mixed together in the required amounts, and crushed in grinding mills. The resulting powder is agitated (shaken) and stored.

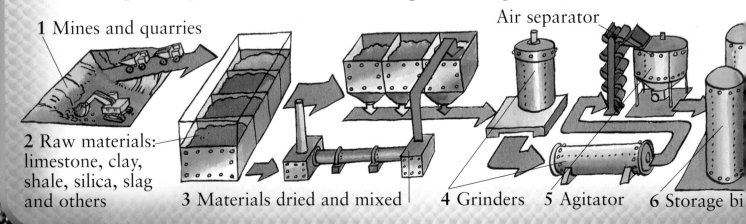

1 Mines and quarries

2 Raw materials: limestone, clay, shale, silica, slag and others

3 Materials dried and mixed

4 Grinders

5 Agitator

Air separator

6 Storage bin

CONCRETE

Cement, water, sand (fine aggregate) and gravel (coarse aggregate) mix to make concrete. Like mortar, this sets hard by chemical action, rather than by drying out. So concrete can be used under water for dams and bridge towers, as well as for a host of other uses such as skyscrapers, tunnels, floors, roadways and wall panels.

Concrete is very hard, but it may crack as it bends. So steel rods or frames are put inside it, for extra strength. This is reinforced concrete.

Ideas for the FUTURE

As concrete's strength is improved, architects can plan skyscrapers which are taller yet slimmer. This design for a Mile-High Tower has a tapering top which seems to disappear into the sky.

A Mile-High Tower?

...he mix is heated in a pipe-shaped ...en or kiln, to make lumpy clinker. ...he mineral gypsum is added and the ...al cement is milled to a powder.

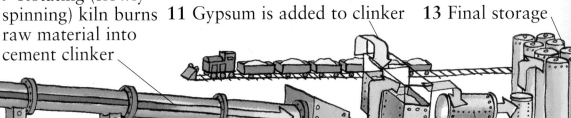

8 Dust is taken away

9 Rotating (slowly spinning) kiln burns raw material into cement clinker

11 Gypsum is added to clinker

13 Final storage

Powder mix

10 Clinker is cooled

12 Cement is milled into powder

Clays are naturally squishy, fine-grained, earthy substances from the ground. Most contain the minerals silica and alumina. They go hard when dry, and even harder if heated in an oven. Clay minerals have been used for thousands of years to make jars, vases, cups, bowls, plates and pots – items known as pottery.

THE MAKING OF A MUG

1 Clay, feldspar, flint particles, water and other raw materials

Water

In many ways, making pottery is similar to cooking. The ingredients are mixed together, with various amounts of clays and other minerals, depending on th type of pottery needed. Extra chemicals are usually included, such as pigments (for colour) and hardeners Much of the skill lies in knowing how hot, and how long, to fire or 'cook' the shaped clay in the kiln.

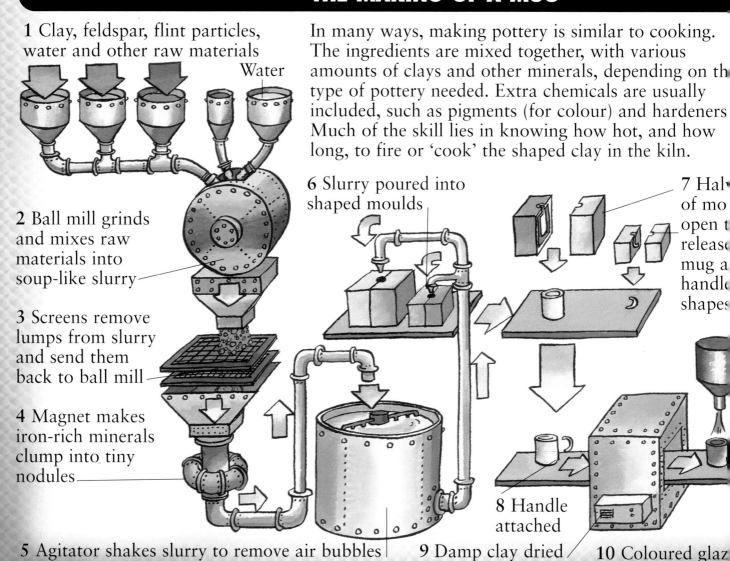

2 Ball mill grinds and mixes raw materials into soup-like slurry

3 Screens remove lumps from slurry and send them back to ball mill

4 Magnet makes iron-rich minerals clump into tiny nodules

6 Slurry poured into shaped moulds

7 Hal of mo open t release mug a handle shapes

8 Handle attached

5 Agitator shakes slurry to remove air bubbles

9 Damp clay dried

10 Coloured glaz

Today pottery is made on a production line. Here tableware is stacked, ready to be decorated either by the application of transfers or printing. A clear glaze is then applied to protect the decoration.

Pottery is one of the oldest crafts, first practised 10,000 years ago in Eastern Asia. Items were practical, but also decorated with colours and designs. Pictures on ancient pots, plates and bowls help us to understand history by showing people and scenes from long ago.

An Ancient Greek pottery vase.

...orcester porcelain ...a set. Porcelain is ...ade from a special ...pe of clay, kaolin ...hina clay). This ...ntains the mineral ...ldspar. Porcelain is ...ry hard and shiny, ...d items can be ...ade so thin, they ...e translucent ...lmost see-through).

Making items on a potter's wheel has hardly changed for thousands of years.

SHAPED AND BAKED

Only certain kinds of clays are suitable for pottery. Different clays from various quarries may be mixed or blended, and water added to make them into a paste. Items are shaped on a slowly-spinning potter's wheel or in moulds. Then they are baked, or fired, in a kiln (oven) to make them hard. They may be covered by a mixture of glass-making minerals before firing, to form a hard, shiny covering, called the glaze.

Mug fired in kiln

19

Clay-rich soils and minerals have many uses, such as making bricks and pots, as shown on previous pages. The general name for objects made from clay is ceramics.

HIGH-TECH CERAMICS

In addition to being the product of the ancient craft of pottery, ceramics have many modern uses. To make these objects, clays are blended and mixed with various other minerals and substances, then heated to more than 1,500°C in high-temperature kilns.

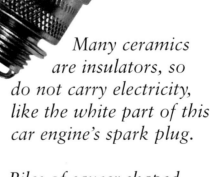

Many ceramics are insulators, so do not carry electricity, like the white part of this car engine's spark plug.

Piles of saucer-shaped ceramic insulators keep high-power cables apart, so the electricity does not leak between them or into the ground.

Many ceramics withstand enormous heat. They are used a linings in furnaces an kilns, and as tiles on the space shuttle.

Flexible fibres like glass-fibre have great strength against bending, but they are not very hard. Ceramics are very hard but, if bent, they crack. A ceramic–fibre composite combines the best features of each.

CLAY COMBINATIONS

Composites are combinations of ceramics with other materials, such as metals like steel, other minerals, glass or carbon-fibre. Each type of composite has its own special features. Ceramic–metal composites are incredibly hard, ideal for bearings and other moving parts in high-speed machines. Ceramic–fibre composites, light but tough, resist heat and make fireproof clothing.

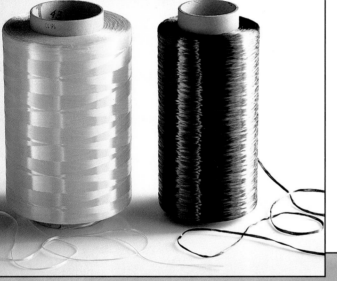

Natural mineral oils can be made into another high-tech material – strong, hard-wearing aramide, used for sails and hang-glider wings.

Ideas for the FUTURE

Metal power cables let through most electricity, but resist a small amount. Ceramic–metal composite cables may become 'super-conductors' with no resistance at all, saving much electrical energy.

Overhead power cables.

A familiar crystal substance is commo salt, obtained from rocks or after sea water dries. The crystals are 'grains'.

Most minerals occur naturally in the form of crystals. These have flat sides, angled edges and sharp corners. Crystals have many amazing features and uses.

OLD AND NEW

From ancient times, people have been fascinated by the shapes, colours and beauty of crystals. Some people believe crystals have mysterious powers to heal illness. Crystals are used in scientific ways, too, to change electricity into vibrations or light.

Facts from the PAST

Scientist Pierre Curie discovered that when electricity is passed through a crystal, it changes shape slightly. The reverse also happens, so that when a crystal is squeezed, it produces a tiny pulse of electricity. This is known as the piezoelectric effect.

Pierre Curie (1859–1906).

Some crystals alter how light passes through them, and are used in the liquid crystal display, LCD.

The mineral quartz, a type of silica, forms large, clear crystals. These are polished int 'crystal balls' which ar supposed to show the future.

Microchips are made from silicon, found in the mineral quartz. Crystals of quartz are made in laboratory pressure tanks, shaped into rods, purified and sliced into wafers. Each wafer receives a coating sensitive to ultraviolet light, which shines through a stencil with the shapes of the electronic micro-components. Acid chemicals remove the coating to leave the micro-circuits on the wafer or 'chip'.

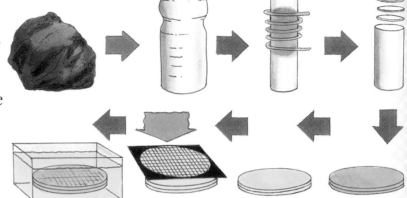

1 Quartz (silica) mineral is grown in laboratory as crystal

2 Silica is purified and sliced into thin wafers

5 Acid removes coating to leave electronic circuit

4 Ultraviolet light shines through stencil

3 Wafer coated with special covering

COMPUTER CRYSTALS

The mineral quartz contains silicon and oxygen (SiO_2). It occurs in many forms in nature – including sand. Quartz crystals are used in clocks, computers and electronic equipment. Quartz is also a raw material for making glass.

This enlarged view shows many microchips on a thin slice of the mineral silicon.

Crystals bend or deflect waves and rays, including light waves and X-rays. This feature is used in the scientific laboratory test called X-ray crystallography.

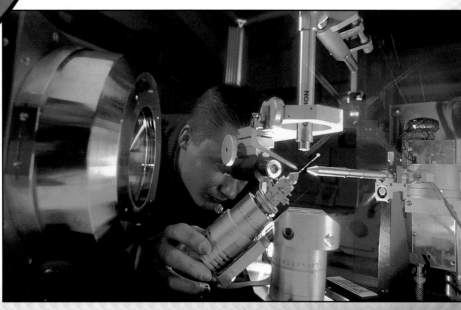

Some of the most precious objects in the world are minerals dug out from rocks. They are jewels or gem 'stones', that glow or glint with beautiful colours.

SIMPLE SUBSTANCES

Most jewels and gems, like diamonds, rubies, sapphires and emeralds, are crystals of natural minerals. And most contain simple chemical substances. Diamond contains only carbon – the same substance that, in a different form, makes up soot. Red rubies and blue sapphires are both crystals of the mineral corundum, which contains only aluminium and oxygen (Al_2O_3).

Only a few types of rocks contain gems. The 'Big Hole' is an old, dug-out diamond mine near Kimberley, South Africa.

1 Diamond-containing kimberlite rock

2 Rock loosened, broken up and loaded on to wagons

Most gems, like these rubies, are found in the rocks as rough, dull-looking lumps. Only when cut and polished, do they shine with great colour

WHY SO PRECIOUS?

If jewels and gems contain only simple mineral substances, why are they so valuable? Partly because they are rare, so owning one is a symbol of wealth and power. Most are also very hard and long-lasting – diamond is the hardest natural substance. And they can be cut and polished, to shine and sparkle.

…amonds have many industrial …es, such as teeth on drill bits.

MINING AND PROCESSING DIAMONDS

…ually, a lump of rock bigger than a house …ust be crushed and sorted, to find one …all gem. In a typical diamond mine, the …ck is loosened by explosives or drills. It is …rried by wagons or trucks to huge …shers, which pound it to a powder and …x it with water as a slurry.

A large paddle stirs the slurry in a tank. The heavier diamond-containing pieces sink to the bottom and pass on to a moving belt coated with sticky grease. High-pressure jets of water wash away the remaining unwanted particles, leaving rough diamonds. These are freed by melting the grease.

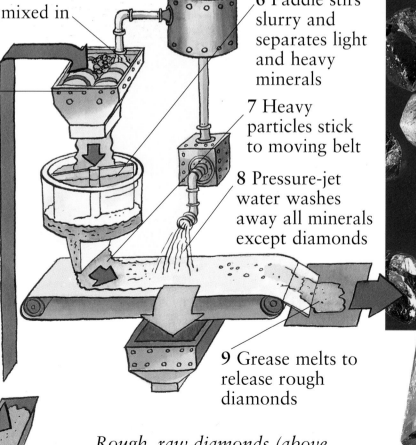

…Rock …ces and …ter are fed …o main …nding mill

…Rock …ken into …aller …ces by …sher

5 Water mixed in

6 Paddle stirs slurry and separates light and heavy minerals

7 Heavy particles stick to moving belt

8 Pressure-jet water washes away all minerals except diamonds

9 Grease melts to release rough diamonds

Rough, raw diamonds (above right) and cut, polished diamond (right)

Rocks and minerals are not only important for construction, factories and industries. They are needed for the healthy growth of crops, farm animals – and humans.

STAYING HEALTHY

The human body needs a regular supply of certain minerals to grow, especially for strong bones and teeth. Usually there are plenty of these minerals in our food. But in some cases, tablets called supplements help to supply any missing minerals.

Mineral fertilizers are first tested in the laboratory (left). If they are safe and do little harm to the environment, they can be made in bulk and spread on the land (above).

In some illnesses, the body cannot take in enough minerals from food. Mineral supplement tablets help boost supplies.

Facts from the **PAST**

Before fertilizers were made in factories, people used natural sources of minerals for their crops. One very rich source was guano. This is the huge piles of droppings from sea birds, bats and other animals that live packed together in colonies. Mining guano was difficult and dangerous – and very smelly! Factory-made fertilizers began to take over in the 1920s.

Mining guano on an island off Peru, 1863.

MAKING MINERAL-RICH FERTILIZER

Three important types of minerals for plants are nitrates, phosphates and the substance potassium. These come from rocks and man-made chemicals.

The raw materials are mixed in huge water-cooled tanks. The result is a soup-like fertilizer slurry, which is dried to a powder and put into bags.

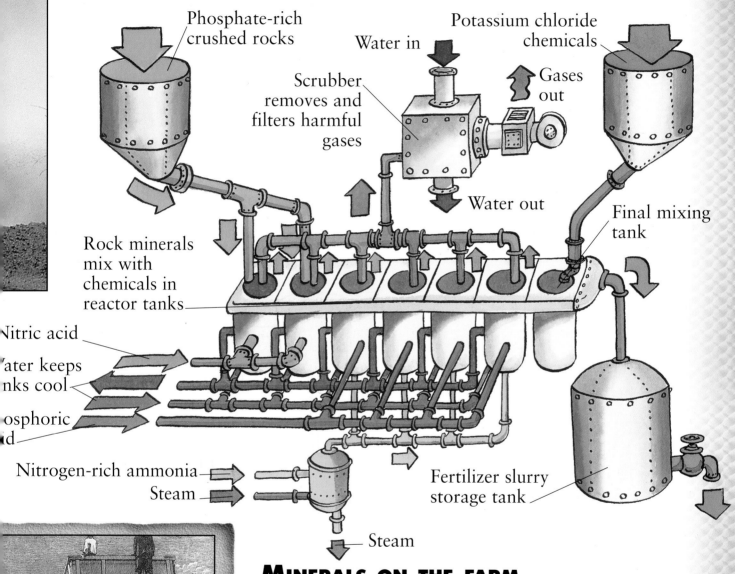

Phosphate-rich crushed rocks

Potassium chloride chemicals

Water in

Scrubber removes and filters harmful gases

Gases out

Water out

Final mixing tank

Rock minerals mix with chemicals in reactor tanks

Nitric acid

Water keeps tanks cool

Phosphoric acid

Nitrogen-rich ammonia

Steam

Fertilizer slurry storage tank

Steam

MINERALS ON THE FARM

Like people, farm animals such as sheep, cows and pigs need regular supplies of minerals in their feed, for healthy growth. Crops like wheat and rice require certain mixtures of minerals, too. These may occur naturally in the soil, or farmers can improve crop growth using mineral-rich fertilizers.

Will rocks and minerals last into the future? The Earth is so vast that there seem to be endless supplies of them. But one main problem is the way we mine, quarry and process them.

THE NEED FOR ENERGY

Mines and quarries have huge machines with diesel engines or electric motors. These use up lots of energy. Also, cutting stone blocks, finding gems, baking ceramics, making cement, and processing fertilizers all need great amounts of energy. Supplies of oil, coal and other energy fuels may run out long before rocks and minerals do.

Coal from mines (above) and oil from drilling rigs (left) are minerals, forme in the Earth by natural processes long ago.

Acid rain pollution damages even hard stone.

Ideas for the FUTURE

Could we obtain valuable minerals fro other places in the Solar System? Perhaps. Six Apollo space missions, with 12 astronauts, visited the Moon from 1969 to 1972. They brought bac almost 400 kilograms of Moon rocks and dust. But the cost of the missions was so great that the Moon rocks wer far more valuable, for their weight, th the finest diamonds. Space-mining is very unlikely in the foreseeable future.

E-USE AND RECYCLING

here are many ways we can help to ve rocks, minerals and energy for e future. Old building blocks and icks can be cleaned and used again new buildings, or crushed and put to building foundations. Precious inerals and their products, such as ramics and glass, can be recycled ther than thrown away.

ning minerals in space – a distant dream?

In some areas, rocks are plentiful on the ground. These can be skilfully built into environmentally friendly stone walls.

MAKING CRYSTALS

Many rocks containing crystals and gems have already been mined. It is more difficult to find new sources. However, some crystals can be made by machines. Ruby crystals are valuable in jewellery (see page 24), and also in high-tech equipment such as lasers. They are a form of the mineral corundum, which is made up of aluminium and oxygen. Raw materials containing these substances are made into rubies using heat and pressure.

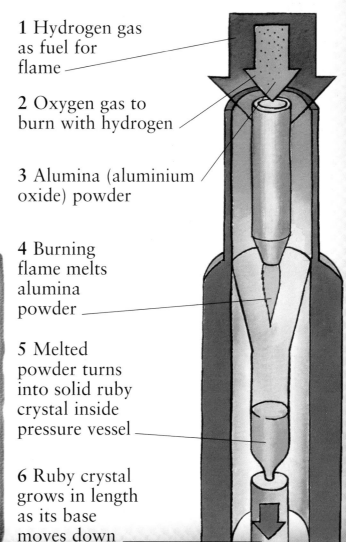

1 Hydrogen gas as fuel for flame

2 Oxygen gas to burn with hydrogen

3 Alumina (aluminium oxide) powder

4 Burning flame melts alumina powder

5 Melted powder turns into solid ruby crystal inside pressure vessel

6 Ruby crystal grows in length as its base moves down

TYPE OF ROCK		FEATURES AND USES
IGNEOUS	Granite	Very hard rock with large grains or crystals, usually in whites, greys, pinks and yellows; used for building blocks and slabs
	Gabbro	Crumbly rock with large grey-green crystals; source of copper
	Basalt	Dark, small grains; crushed for road and railway foundations
	Obsidian	Hard, dark, glassy; used for jewellery, decorations, sculpture
	Pumice	Very light weight and colour, soft and crumbly, almost spongy; used to retain heat, as a soft abrasive and in chemical processe
	Porphyry	Mixture of large pale and small dark grains; used for building
	Granophyre	Speckled pink, white and black; used in decorative gravel path
SEDIMENTARY	Chalk	Whitish, fairly soft, powdery form of limestone (below), made mainly of tiny fossils; used for drawing and marking
	Limestone	Varies greatly, usually white or pale with mixed grains and perhaps fossils; used for decorative slabs, walls, blocks, statues
	Flint	Usually nodules (lumps) in other rocks such as chalk, colours vary from black to white; splits to give very sharp edges
	Tuff	Rock made of fine volcanic fragments; soft, easily carved
	Dolomite	Light pink, grey or yellow, with tiny grains or crystals; often contains oil (petroleum), used for building blocks
	Pudding stone	Large pebbles in fine grey powder; looks like natural concrete
METAMORPHIC	Mica schist	Multicoloured streaks and lumps; used for bright decoration
	Gneiss	Mix of light and dark grains; used as blocks and polished slab
	Slate	Greyish, splits into thin sheets; used for roof tiles
	Marble	Beautiful streaks and swirls in many colours, easily shaped; used for statues, paving slabs, tiles, blocks and decoration

GLOSSARY

earing

rt of a machine, which reduces
ction to allow free movement
tween two moving parts.

hemical element

pure substance, which cannot be
oken up into any simpler
bstances. Oxygen, aluminium
d iron are all chemical elements.

ectronic circuit

n arrangement of the parts that
ake computers function.

vironment

he surroundings, including water,
, soil, rocks, plants and animals.

rosion

earing down and breaking up of
cks into smaller pieces, by forces
nature such as the wind, sun,
in, ice, snow and running water.

cavator

large mechanical digger, used
r removing rocks and soil from
e ground.

firing

Heating or baking clay pots and
other ceramic materials in ovens or
kilns, so that they go very hard.

geologist

A scientist who studies rocks,
minerals, the forces which shape
the landscape, and the Earth itself.

kiln

A large oven in which pottery or
bricks are fired.

mass produced

Made in large quantities and
identical shapes.

micro-circuit

An extremely small electronic
circuit with parts formed in just
one microchip.

production line

A moving line in a factory. Parts
are gradually added to the product
being made as it moves along the
line, until it is completed at the
end of the line.